Moth Orchid Mastery

Raffaele Di Lallo

CONTENTS

1 A NOTE FROM THE AUTHOR

First and foremost, thank you for purchasing this book and I am confident that you will gain an abundance of valuable information from reading this book! If you have been frustrated with moth orchid culture, or are just a complete novice at growing them, then this is the book for you! This is a very informative and concise book that I've written based off of many years of experience in growing Moth Orchids.

I would recommend reading through the entirety of this book first, and then circle back to specific chapters to reinforce specific topics.

Disclaimer: This is NOT a picture book, so if you want a book with pretty photos, there are many of those out there. The main intent of this book is for me to arm you with all the valuable cultural tips that will be useful for ANYONE to easily grow these gorgeous plants that we know as Moth Orchids, or the Phalaenopsis genus. However, I do realize that photos ARE important to illustrate certain concepts and procedures, so you can refer to a few of my blog posts from www.ohiotropics.com that DO have photos if you'd like.

I hope you enjoy this book, and if you have any questions at all, you can contact me with any questions at theohiotropics@gmail.com. You can also subscribe to my houseplant blog at www.ohiotropics.com with your email, as well as follow my daily photos and tips on Instagram (@ohiotropics). I am very active on Instagram and offer many tips about houseplant care in general, but you can also find me on Facebook (Ohio Tropics Blog) and Twitter (@ohiotropicsblog) as well. However, I am most active on Instagram by far.

Lastly, if you enjoy this book, please spread the word to your friends and family and be sure to leave me a review on Amazon!

Kind Regards,

Raffaele Di Lallo
Ohio Tropics

I understand why everyone is so terrified of growing orchids. They ARE fundamentally different from your typical houseplant after all. I've heard of so many people that simply throw them out after they are done blooming! The horror! Moth orchids, or Phalaenopsis, have a totally undeserved reputation of being finicky, difficult to rebloom, and disposable plants after they are done blooming.

But this really could not be further from the truth! I've heard so many friends, family members and strangers struggle with growing these plants, but at the same time, my plants have flourished and bloomed with ease and minimal effort.

After I started giving moth orchid cultural advice to many people, and hearing about how I've helped them successfully grow and rebloom their orchids, I became very encouraged. Especially when they were so excited and in disbelief that they were able to rebloom them once my advice was followed.

This led me to start my blog site www.ohiotropics.com in March of 2017 and my first post was actually about growing moth orchids. I've always had a special place in my heart for orchids. They have such an elusive, mysterious history, and I read about orchid hunting and orchid collecting long before I started growing them. My blog site started quite abruptly after I received a phone call from my friend Donna. She declared that I needed to start a blog site to share all my botanical wisdom. In proper Raffaele fashion, when I get excited about something, I started researching with all guns blazing. Shortly after that phone call, I launched my blog.

It became easier after writing a few blog posts because I would simply refer people to my blog posts, instead of having to regurgitate the details every single time someone asked me questions about growing moth orchids. Then as my blog audience grew, and my Instagram account started to explode (@ohiotropics), I decided to take it a step further and write this short book.

There is so much misinformation out there, as well as information that just lacks the clarity that we all need to understand how to properly grow plants. So many sites that seemingly have the same information; some of it erroneous, and much of it not catered to the average houseplant grower. And there are so few sources that actually seem to be speaking from personal experience!

The information in my book is all tried and true information. I speak from personal experience. Proven experience that has helped countless people discover that moth orchids are truly a joy to grow and rebloom.

So, with courage of conviction, I embarked on a journey to write this book. It is my mission to provide all the basic information that you need to successfully grow these beautiful plants. And it is my mission to demonstrate to you, if you follow my advice, that once you learn a few basic things, YOU TOO can easily learn to rebloom these beauties, and do so for many years to come!

But beware...once the orchid bug bites, there is no turning back.

3 THE ORCHID MYSTIQUE

One day, I walked into Trader Joe's for some groceries, and I found myself schooling a couple of older ladies on how to grow moth orchids. I must admit, I always inspect and admire the moth orchids on sale at any store. I'm drawn to them like a magnet. In fact, I don't even have to think about it. I just start walking toward the orchids! For me, they are a bit like a bag of potato chips. It's very difficult to stop at just one! And once you get orchid fever, it becomes a force to reckon with. Especially once you realize, once and for all, that they ARE easy to grow despite what you may have read or heard.

I can't tell you how many times the following scenario has happened:

Enter Ohio Tropics into Trader Joe's grocery store. Two middle-aged women are spotted hovering over the moth orchid display and contemplating purchasing plants.

Lady #1: (Turns her head to Lady #2) Oh look at those moth orchids! Aren't they lovely!

Lady #2: Oh they're stunning. But aren't they hard to take care of? I've killed so many of them and I can't get them to rebloom!

Lady #1: Oh supposedly all you need to do is give them 3 ice cubes a week. But mine never did very well either so I really don't know...

After quietly stalking the two ladies, Ohio Tropics encroaches into the moth orchid display to offer some advice.

Ohio Tropics: The ice cubes are your issue. That's just a marketing gimmick and you'll be doomed to fail if you water any plant that way! I can explain the proper way to water your moth orchids. I like to take mine to the kitchen sink and thoroughly soak them. I actually wrote a few blog posts on caring for these plants.

Lady #1 and #2 eagerly nod their heads. Ohio Tropics reaches into his pocket to take out two business cards and hands them to the ladies.

Ohio Tropics: Here is my business card. Visit www.ohiotropics.com and read my blog posts. They are really SO easy to take care of once you understand them!

Lady #1: Thank you so much! I'm going to try again!

Lady #2: Oh thank you! You've inspired me to try again too.

Lady #1 and #2 each pick out another moth orchid and place them in their shopping carts. Ohio Tropics walks away and continues his grocery shopping.

Maybe that's why so many people have such bad luck with growing moth orchids! No one should be watering any plants with ice. The cold ice cubes can damage the tropical plant's roots, and you will not achieve a good soaking of the potting media. There is so much misinformation out there on moth orchids.

The truth of the matter is that moth orchids, or Phalaenopsis, truly ARE very easy to grow once you understand their needs. It is my personal goal, through this book, to help you realize how easy these plants are to care for.

Throughout this book, I will explain in a very accessible way, how to care for these exotic beauties so that they can thrive in your home. If you have failed at growing these plants in the past, you will realize what you did wrong after you finish reading this book. I have taught countless people how to care for and rebloom these remarkable plants.

I have people messaging me daily on my Instagram account (@ohiotropics) and through my blog site www.ohiotropics.com, where I write about general houseplant care, that they have finally been able to rebloom their orchids.

All of this keeps me going, so let me teach YOU how easy it really is!

When you select your moth orchid for purchase, there are a few critical things that you should be looking for.

ROOTS

The roots should be healthy, firm and plump. Visually inspect the roots and make sure that they are not shriveled or soft. They should appear a greyish white or greenish color. It is OK if you see roots coming out of the top of the pot. This does not indicate that anything is wrong with your orchid!

Moth orchids, like most orchids, are epiphytes in nature so they grow on other plants such as trees. Many of their roots are exposed to the air. Many times, moth orchids are grown in clear plastic containers and slipped into a more decorative pot. In those cases, pull out the clear plastic container and inspect the health of the roots before you make the purchase.

LEAVES

The leaves should be firm and a healthy green color. Depending on how much light the plants have received, the leaves can be anywhere from a light green to a dark green color. Sometimes you might see a reddish tinge to the edge of the leaves. This is OK and just indicates that the plant has been grown at the higher end of its light tolerance.

FLOWERS

Last but not least, inspect the flowers! This is why you are buying the plant in the first place, right? Ideally, all of the flowers should NOT be open. Sometimes you just can't avoid this though so don't let that stop you from buying the plant. If all of the flowers are open, it is hard to know how long they have been open for and they will not last as long for you when you take the plant home. Try and select a plant that has flowers open at the bottom of the flower stalk, but still has a few unopened buds near the tip of the stalk. Check the unopened buds to make sure that they are not shriveled or brown.

At least where I live, Phalaenopsis orchids are found in abundance in grocery stores, hardware stores, garden centers and other locations. They tend to be much cheaper in large hardware stores and even grocery stores. I try not to pay any more than $15 or so for a single plant. They are so plentiful that this is usually never a problem. I also can't help myself when the orchids go out of bloom and stores place them on sale. Time to collect more! Garden centers and florists will tend to be much more expensive, so I tend not to purchase them at those locations. But sometimes it is worth paying more for an exceptional specimen.

This is the most important chapter of this book, so please take everything I say here to heart. Every chapter is important, but this topic in particular will determine if your moth orchid will rebloom for you. No one buys a moth orchid for its foliage, so read this carefully!

There are so many misconceptions in general on what the appropriate light is for any houseplant. Providing your plant with adequate light should be your first and foremost consideration when you are placing any houseplant in your home. After all, plants use light to photosynthesize and make food for themselves. Deprive them of light, and deprive them of food! Especially flowering plants since they tend to need more light, in general, than many foliage plants.

DISPLAYING YOUR ORCHID

First of all, before anything else, you must place your moth orchid where you can enjoy it! Otherwise why bother? Whether you just purchased your moth orchid in bloom, or you have just rebloomed it yourself, place it somewhere where you can enjoy it while it is in bloom!

I place most of my moth orchids on display in the house while they are blooming. It is perfectly acceptable to place them on display, even if it's not in a location where it should be growing permanently. I've made it my duty to accumulate so many moth orchids that I have at LEAST one in bloom at ALL times! And I have achieved this goal!

When my moth orchids are blooming I place them all over the house in areas such as on top of:

The table in the foyer

My piano

The coffee table in the living room

The buffet in the dining room

The kitchen table

Anywhere you can think of! Just avoid areas that are completely dark, or conversely, areas that have a lot of direct sun. We'll get into that shortly. It will do no harm at all to have the blooming plants on display temporarily where you can enjoy them. As long as you return them to their proper permanent growing location when they are done blooming.

LIGHT FOR YOUR ORCHID

Phalaenopsis, or moth orchids, are among the lower light orchids. One misconception that many people have in general about houseplants is the light designation commonly found on the plastic identification tags when you purchase your plant. How are you supposed to decipher that information? Low light? Medium light? High light? What does all of this really mean?

Oh, the tag says low light so I can take my plant and shove it in that dark corner over there. Right? Wrong. So wrong. Although moth orchids are among some of the lower light orchids, they still need a good amount of light in order to grow, and most importantly, bloom for you!

FINDING A WINDOW FOR YOUR MOTH ORCHID

Although you can certainly grow orchids under lights, this topic is not discussed in this book. I will focus on natural light only.

Did you notice that I put the word "window" in the subtitle? There are very few plants that I would place too far from a window. Moth orchids are definitely plants that should be (except for when you have them on display), right in front of a window! And by right in front, I'm talking about within 2 feet or less from the window, unless you are fortunate enough to have a gigantic wall of windows. You may have a little more leeway there. The intensity of light drops DRASTICALLY the further you move away from a window, so even a couple of feet can sometimes make a big difference.

I've found that moth orchids grow extremely well for me in front of Eastern exposure windows. This exposure will get morning sun which is gentle enough for these orchids in most cases. I like to call Eastern exposure windows a good "catch-all" window. They may provide the high end of light tolerance for "low light" plants, but also provide a minimum light exposure for "high light" plants to grow well. So, you can grow a nice variety of plants in front of Eastern exposure windows.

If you have any African Violets that are thriving and blooming where they are, moth orchids will likely love that spot as well!

In general, moth orchids don't like a lot of direct sun, but some is certainly OK. Especially if it is the gentler morning sunshine that Eastern exposure windows offer.

North windows typically get little, if any, direct light. This exposure may be OK for your moth orchids, especially if it is a large North window, but I still prefer Eastern exposure. You may wish to experiment and monitor your plant. Better yet, go buy several moth orchids and experiment with window locations!

Light is a pretty complicated topic. I have a couple moth orchids in front of a wall of Northern windows, but the room also has a skylight and small wall of East windows. Those orchids rebloom for me with no problem.

If all you have are Western and Southern exposure windows, you'll need to diffuse the direct sun because these exposures will be too harsh for your moth orchids. You can do one of a few things:

Set your plant a little further back from the window

Use blinds to diffuse the direct sun

Use sheer curtains to diffuse the direct sun

OTHER LIGHT CONSIDERATIONS

Keep in mind that what works for one person, may not work for others! So be weary of information that is too specific. There are so many factors that affect how much light your plant will get:

Obstructions by your window such as trees or buildings

Size of the window

Type of window glass

Your geographical location

The season of the year

Depending on some of the above factors, you may or may not need to use blinds or sheer curtains for your West or South window. Or conversely, you may have a small North window with a huge tree in front of it. This will likely not be a suitable spot for your moth orchid. Or maybe your location for your plant is OK in the winter, but then in the summer, the light will be too strong.

So how do you know if your moth orchid is receiving too little or too much light?

TOO LITTLE LIGHT

The number one factor by far for a moth orchid not blooming is inadequate light! How can you tell if your moth orchid is not receiving enough light? If the leaves are a deep, dark green, chances are that your plant is not receiving enough light. It may survive just fine and even continue to grow new leaves, but it will certainly not bloom again for you. You will notice that the leaves will turn a lighter shade of green if you move it to a brighter location.

TOO MUCH LIGHT

Moth orchids cannot tolerate a lot of strong, direct sun. In nature, they'll receive indirect light, or dappled shade mostly. Phalaenopsis are epiphytes which means that they grow on other plants, such as on tree branches. They do not sit in wide open spaces in baking sun all day.

How can you tell if your Phalaenopsis is getting too much light? The first indication is that the leaves will start to turn reddish around the edges. If you see this, it should not be cause for alarm, but it is telling you that your plant is close to the maximum end of its light tolerance. In more extreme cases, if your plant is exposed to too much direct sun, the leaves will burn and develop unsightly yellow and brown spots on the leaves.

Just monitor your plants carefully and it will tell you if it is getting the light that it needs based off of how the leaves look and if your plant is reblooming.

Before I get into proper watering and fertilizing of your moth orchid, let me start by dispelling a watering myth. It is one of the most ridiculous things that I've heard of when it comes to plant care. Are you ready?

It is the method of using ice cubes to water your orchid. Ice cubes. Really? First of all, unless you see a monkey sashaying around the tropics with a raspberry popsicle, I'd like you to stay away from using ice cubes to water your orchid. I've seen tags on moth orchids at the store that say to simply "water" your orchid once a week with 3 ice cubes. There are so many things wrong with this:

> First of all, plant care is not formulaic. I will never recommend to someone to water all their plants exactly once a week, and with exactly three ice cubes. Everyone's conditions are different, and thus water requirements will be different. Differences in light levels, temperature, the season, etc., all play a part in how much water a plant will need.

> Secondly, ice should not make it anywhere near these plants. These are tropical plants and ice can potentially damage the roots. In addition, the melting ice cubes will not provide enough water to thoroughly soak the potting media.

WATERING YOUR MOTH ORCHID

Unlike some other types of orchids such as cattleyas that have pseudobulbs for water storage, moth orchids do not have these. They must never completely dry out if you can help it. The potting media should be allowed to almost dry out, but not completely. Then at that point, you should give your plant a thorough watering.

I take each and every one of my moth orchids straight to the kitchen or bathroom sink and soak them thoroughly when they need to be watered. I use plain, tepid tap water and run the water out of the faucet or my watering can for a good 15-30 seconds. I also turn the pot to make sure that I'm soaking every bit of the potting media.

Also, your Phalaenopsis might have some wild roots that are growing above the potting medium and that is perfectly OK! In nature, these plants use their roots to attach onto tree trunks or branches, as well as to absorb moisture from the air. And of course, they also gather moisture and nutrients from when it rains. So be sure to moisten these roots too, otherwise over time you will find that they will dry up and shrivel away.

Some people like to water their orchids using the following method. And it is a great one as well! This method conserves water, which is always a good thing. If you have a plant that is growing in a plastic pot with drainage holes, and you have it slipped into a decorative pot with no drainage holes, you can simply fill the decorative pot with water and let the plant sit for a few minutes to absorb water. Then lift the plastic pot out, discard the excess water, and slip the plastic pot back into the decorative pot. Don't forget to drain the water out though otherwise you will quickly rot your plant out!

One word of caution though! Be sure that you don't get water stuck in the crown of the plant, or between where the leaves are attached to the base of the plant. If water sits here for an extended period of time, especially with cooler temperatures, your plant may rot. Inevitably as you water, you will get water in these locations. To remedy that, I simply hold my face right up to the plant, take a deep breath, and blow the water out. Or if you prefer, you can take a paper towel or kitchen towel and use it to gently blot the water out.

SIGNS THAT YOU ARE UNDERWATERING

Some signs that you are underwatering your moth orchid include:

> The lower leaves will turn yellow and start to go limp and be wrinkly. If you see this, you'll know that you're going to have to up your watering game. If the lower leaves are just slightly wrinkled, they may recover once you start a good watering regiment. In extreme cases, you will lose the lower leaves. If they turn completely yellow, you'll have to cut the leaves off.

> The roots are firm, but look shriveled and aren't round and plump.

> You might experience bud blasting. Which means that the flower buds may be drying up and falling off instead of continuing to grow and open.

SIGNS THAT YOU ARE OVERWATERING

Some signs that you have overwatered your moth orchid include:

> The potting media might have a rancid odor.

> The plant may be wobbly in the pot, indicating that its roots have rotted and no longer have a firm grounding in the pot to remain stable.

The roots might be mushy, and if you pull on them, the outer part of the roots will just slide off and reveal a string in the middle of the root. This indicates root rot.

Similar to underwatering, you may also get bud blasting if you are overwatering.

WATER QUALITY

Many people have asked me about what kind of water they should be using to water orchids and various other plants. When I tell them I just use tap water, many are shocked because it is not the best water to use. While this is true, I have too many plants in general to water with anything else, so most of the time, I use water straight out of the tap.

The only time that you definitely should not be using tap water is if you are using a water softener. If you have a water softening system in your home, you can NOT use this on any plants because the sodium content in softened water is very toxic to plants.

The best water to use though, assuming your area is not heavily polluted, is rain water. Nature does it best right? Rain water actually has more nitrogen in it, and this is a necessary macronutrient for all plants and will help encourage healthy leaf growth! But if you are like me, using tap water is perfectly OK and has provided me with great results.

FREQUENCY OF WATERING

Another myth I'd like to dispel is the notion that all plants need to be watered once a week. Although this would make it simple for us if we pick a day of the week and water only on that day, it's not always the best thing to follow. Granted, it MAY work for you, but not always! Many factors affect how much water a plant uses: light levels, temperature, pot size, type of pot, humidity, etc.

The vast majority of moth orchids that you would purchase grow in either a bark chunk mix, or in sphagnum moss. Most of my plants are growing in a bark mix made specifically for Phalaenopsis orchids. I do have a handful that grow in Sphagnum moss though. More on this topic in the Repotting chapter. My point is that the ones that grow in Sphagnum moss, in my personal case, do NOT need to be watered weekly. They stay moist enough that I sometimes wait 2 weeks or more before watering again.

The moral of the story is that you should not rely on your calendar to tell you when to water a plant. You should water a plant when it needs to be watered! I like to use my finger and feel the surface of the potting media. You'll need to water when the top inch or two of the potting media feels dry. At the same time, you don't want to allow the whole potting media to dry out completely. Phalaenopsis have no water storing pseudobulbs like many other orchids do, so they don't tolerate drought well.

The type of pot also makes a huge difference on the frequency of watering. I would not recommend terra cotta pots for moth orchids because they dry out much too quickly. My preferred type of pot for moth orchids are clear plastic pots because you can actually see how dry the roots are and can also monitor the root health. This is just personal preference though and many scenarios are possible.

Lastly, whatever you do, make sure that your moth orchid is never sitting in water for extended periods of time. This will quickly rot out your plant. All epiphytes are very sensitive to this. Because of the way they grow in nature, they demand excellent drainage and a porous potting media.

Finally, I'm about to say something that may shock you. Especially if you do follow me closely on my @ohiotropics Instagram page, or my blog at www.ohiotropics.com, where I preach about my watering techniques. I would NEVER say this for a houseplant growing in soil indoors. And I would NEVER say this for a moth orchid growing in sphagnum moss indoors. However, if your orchid is growing in a bark mix indoors, as a starting point, you CAN water it once a week and then make any tweaks needed from there. Make sure that you water it using the methods I describe in this chapter however.

In 99.9% of all cases, I would never recommend a certain frequency of watering any plant indoors. This is the only exception. Orchids growing in bark chunks have extremely well drained and airy growing conditions for their roots, so you can start by watering your moth orchid this way. If you need to adjust, you definitely can. Since moth orchids are so different from many other plants (especially from plants that grow in soil), you can treat them a little differently. And I know some people like to keep schedules for watering. I'm normally not a fan at all for scheduled watering for quite a few reasons, but for moth orchids growing in a bark mix, it will likely be good enough! I'm excluding plants that are outdoors for the summer. This paragraph would not apply. You may need much more frequent watering depending on the temperature and other conditions.

FERTILIZING YOUR MOTH ORCHID

There are so many different fertilizers out there that it can be very confusing to know which type to use, how often to use them, and what strength to use. I will share with you my experience with fertilizers. I will say though that plants can't read labels so you don't necessarily need to use a fertilizer that is labeled just for orchids!

Let me start off by saying that if you have a plant that is sickly, stressed, diseased, or not doing well, you should not turn to fertilizer as your solution. If you do so, you may be doing more damage than good. Fertilizing will not fix or make up for faulty cultural conditions. So hold off on fertilizing until you troubleshoot your plant and it starts to look healthier.

Likewise, if you have allowed your potting media to completely dry out, you should soak your plant first with plain water. Fertilizing a plant, especially with a full strength solution, that has gone bone dry will potentially damage the roots and cause fertilizer burn.

FERTILIZER BASICS

On every fertilizer label, you will see 3 numbers. These 3 numbers are called the NPK ratio. If you have taken chemistry class, this should look familiar as they are the chemical symbols from the Periodic Table of Elements. Each of the 3 letters stands for a chemical symbol:

The first letter, N, is Nitrogen. Nitrogen fuels the growth of leaves.

The second letter, P, is Phosphorous. Phosphorous helps with root growth and flowering. If you see "bloom booster" fertilizers, these always have a higher Phosphorous proportion. The Phosphorous is actually expressed as phosphate.

The last letter, K, is Potassium. Potassium helps with overall biological functions of plant growth as well as bolsters disease resistance. Potassium is expressed as potash.

If you see a fertilizer labeled 10-15-10, it is telling you:

The proportion of Nitrogen is 10% by weight

The proportion of Phosphorous is 15% by weight

The proportion of Potassium is 10% by weight

Old conventional orchid growing wisdom has always said that if you grow orchids in bark mix, that you should use a 30-10-10 fertilizer. The reason is that the decomposing bark will consume a lot of nitrogen, and hence the higher proportion of nitrogen. However, I can tell you that I've never used this type of fertilizer and even experts now say that 30-10-10 is not necessary. My current choice of fertilizer for my moth orchids is a 20-20-20 blend made specifically for orchids. Experiment and see what works best for you! If you want to get fancy, you can use a balanced fertilizer like a 20-20-20 during the main growing season, and then use a bloom booster fertilizer while the plant is getting ready to grow a flower stalk. This is not necessary however.

FEEDING YOUR MOTH ORCHIDS

There are a couple different ways to fertilize your orchids. You can:

Option 1: Apply the fertilizer as directed on the label. It will normally give you some kind of frequency such as every 10-14 days.

Option 2: You can dilute the fertilizer even further and fertilize with this solution at every watering.

My preferred method is Option 2. But again, experiment and see what works best for you. One reason that I like this method is that you don't have to remember the last time that you fertilized since you are fertilizing at every watering. The other reason I like this method is that the plant will receive a constant source of nutrients. Although dilute, this is more representative of how moth orchids grow in nature because they'll receive a constant supply of nutrients. You can choose to store premixed fertilizer solution in plastic jugs if you'd like and then use it as needed. I keep many premixed, labeled plastic jugs containing different fertilizer solutions that I use for various plants.

Moth orchids grow in tropical regions in Southeast Asia, the Philippines, and parts of Australia. Therefore, you can imagine what the growing temperatures and humidity should be! It's always good to understand where and how plants grow in nature so that we, as their human caretakers, can best provide for our plants.

TEMPERATURE

As far as temperature goes, Phalaenopsis like it warm. They prefer evening temperatures of at least 60F (about 15.6C) and roughly 75-85F (about 24C-29.4C) or so during the day. Of course, these are ideal temperatures and there is a little leeway on either end. A 10-15F temperature differential between day and night temperatures is very good for the general health of these plants.

One interesting point for moth orchids is that if you expose them to nighttime temperatures of about 55F in the Autumn, it will help initiate the growth of flower spikes. This can be easily accomplished if you take your moth orchid outside for the summer and leave it there until the nighttime temperatures are in the mid-50F for a few weeks. Be sure to watch the forecast closely though and bring your plants indoors promptly if temperatures fall much below 55F.

Summering any houseplants outdoors will really work wonders for your plants! If you have a finicky orchid (and they do exist) that refuses to bloom despite your best efforts, often times if you can provide this temperature differential, your plant will bloom! I've done this in the past and it has never failed to work for me. If you do place your moth orchids outside for the summer, they should be placed in a protected area that receives little or no direct sun otherwise the foliage will burn.

If you buy a moth orchid plant in the middle of winter and it is cold outside, take special care to cover your plant up and get to your car as soon as possible! Don't be surprised when you get home if you experience some bud blasting. Bud blast is when the flower buds shrivel up and fall off. It can have a variety of causes, but shocking the plant with cold temperatures is one way to create bud blast. Bud blast can also be caused by excessive drying of the potting media.

HUMIDITY

Phalaenopsis like a humidity range of 50-80%. With higher humidity though, comes an increased need for good air circulation. Orchids prefer and need good air circulation. So how do you provide higher humidity?

First of all, let me discuss the common practice of misting plants. There is a popular notion that you need to mist your houseplants in order to increase humidity. Humidity is a measure of moisture in the air. The only thing that misting does is wet the leaves. It really does almost nothing to increase humidity. In fact, if you overdo it, you could even cause harm to your plants. You could be encouraging fungal diseases especially if your plants' leaves are wet at night and the air circulation is poor. That being said, if your orchid has exposed roots in the air, you can use a mister to wet those roots occasionally. But don't use the mister to mist the whole plant because you think it'll increase the humidity. It won't.

Here are some better ways to increase the humidity for your moth orchids, or for any houseplant for that matter:

Group your plants together. Plants naturally transpire water, so if you group them together, it will create a little microclimate with higher humidity.

You can place your plant on a tray of pebbles to which water has been added. Keep the water level right below the top of the pebbles. This ensures that the bottom of the pot doesn't touch the water. You never want the bottom of the pot that has drainage holes to sit in water. Moth orchids, like any epiphyte, demand excellent drainage. As the water in the pebbles evaporates, it'll create a microclimate of higher humidity.

You can use a portable humidifier, especially if you live in areas with cold winters and forced air heating systems like I do. Forced air heat results in super dry indoor air. Not only can this wreak havoc on your skin, but also on your plants!

Along with higher humidity comes the need for good air circulation. If you have a ceiling fan, or even a smaller portable fan, it would benefit your orchids if you can move the air around them gently. Good air circulation will keep your orchids healthy and will help to prevent certain diseases. Your moth orchid will most likely be OK even if you don't use a ceiling fan, or other fans, as they are quite tolerant of average indoor conditions. But if you can provide a bit of air circulation, your plant will love you that much more.

8 FLOWERING

Your moth orchid should grow a new flower spike about once a year or so, and most of them will do so in the winter to early spring months. Once a year may not sound like it's often enough, but the flowers will easily last about 3-5 months in most conditions! Not bad, right? Although many moth orchids will grow flower spikes in the winter months, don't be surprised if you see a new flower spike growing in the summer or autumn months as well. Sometimes it is difficult for the beginner to distinguish between a new root and a new flower spike. A flower spike will look a bit like a mitten, whereas a root will be uniformly round at the tip.

After you determine that the mysterious growth at the base of your moth orchid is indeed a new flower spike and not a root, there are a couple things to keep in mind:

> Always keep the plant in the same orientation in relation to the window when your moth orchid is growing a new flower spike! Meaning, never rotate your plant when it is growing a new flower spike. Your flower spike will grow towards the window. After you take it to the sink to water, return it to the window in the same orientation that it was in before. If you turn your plant, the flower spike will grow crooked. Although it is not bad for the plant, it will look a bit strange.

> Allow the flower spike to grow a few inches or so, and then you'll need to support it on the bamboo or plastic stake that the plant came with when you purchased it. It should have come with plastic clips to gently secure the flower stalk against the stake. Be gentle though and don't force anything or the flower stalk may break! As the stalk grows, you can support it with more of the plastic clips. You don't HAVE to support it on a stake, but in most cases, this will be the best way to go unless you want a more natural look. Just make sure that you don't bump up against the flower stalk or buds and cause any damage.

By this point in the book, you now know all the important elements in caring for your Phalaenopsis. All of these elements will influence your plant's health, growth and ability to bloom. Let me recap briefly:

> Light is by far the most important factor in getting your moth orchid to bloom!

> Proper watering is also critical and please don't use ice cubes or water that came out of a water softening system!

Fertilizing should be a regular part of your orchid care routine.

Temperature requirements should not be ignored. Remember that if you have a stubborn orchid, a few weeks of nighttime temperatures of around 55F in the Autumn will help trigger blooming.

Humidity and good air circulation are also important, but moth orchids are quite tolerant of average indoor conditions.

Too many people are so scared to grow moth orchids, but once you understand what they like and need, they are actually some of the easiest houseplants that you will grow! After you have success with your first moth orchid, you will gain the confidence that you need. And once that happens...watch out! Orchids are addictive! Your collection will expand. You will acquire more moth orchids for your collection. And then you will expand your horizons to explore the countless tens of thousands of orchid species and modern hybrids...(insert evil laugh here).

OPTIONS POST-BLOOM

What should you do with your orchid after it is done blooming? You have a few options:

Option 1: You can just leave the whole stem intact and sometimes it will continue to grow and bloom at the tip. I personally never do this, but it is an option. The flower spike may continue to grow some buds at the tip, but the stem will grow longer. It will start to look ungainly and the resulting flowers will be smaller.

Option 2: Snip the bloom spike right above one of the nodes on the spike. You'll see a node every few inches on the flower spike. The nodes are very noticeable on the spike and will look like little bumps covered with a little triangular pointed covering. Count one or two nodes below where the bottom flower was located and snip it right above that node. Be sure that you are not cutting it too close to the node. Sometimes your orchid will branch off with new flower spikes right at the node and it will continue to bloom. This may not always happen though so don't get discouraged if it doesn't work. If you start to see that the whole flower spike is turning brown and drying up, it is time to cut the whole stem off. Sometimes your plant will help you decide at which node you should be snipping. You may even see a flower spike already branching off of the main flowering stem.

Option 3: You can just cut the whole flower stem off after all the flowers are spent. Your plant will thank you. Your moth orchid has just bloomed its heart out for you, and it is time for the plant to grow new leaves and store energy so that it can bloom again next year. You don't want to poop your plant out with continual flowering all the time. Plants need rest too. Take a pair of sharp scissors and snip the whole stalk off. It would be a good idea to sterilize the scissors either in a flame or with rubbing alcohol in order to prevent the spread of any disease. Snip the whole spike off as close to the bottom of the plant as possible, without damaging any leaves.

After this point, your plant should start growing more roots and leaves, if it has not already started to do so. If you've had your plant on display somewhere in your house while in bloom, like I always do, return your plant to a window and let it do its thing. If you've left your plant next to a window during its bloom, then just leave it there. Continue to do your regular watering and fertilizing. Summering your orchid outdoors will work wonders for your plant, but wait until the nighttime temperatures stay consistently above the low 50F range.

After your moth orchid is done blooming, it is the perfect time to repot your orchid! Which takes us to the next chapter...

9 REPOTTING

Many people don't realize that you need to repot moth orchids much more frequently than some of your other houseplants. In fact, most people don't even realize that they need to repot, let alone know how to repot, an orchid! Let me subtly say...YOU NEED TO.

Whether your moth orchid is growing in a bark mix or in sphagnum moss, it will need to be repotted every year or two. I personally don't do it every year. Every other year would be a good rule of thumb, but never repotting is not an option. It will die a slow death...you will become an orchid killer, and I will come hunt you down.

Moth orchids, like the majority of orchids, are epiphytes in nature, so they are not terrestrial plants that grow in the soil in the ground. They grow attached to other plants, especially on tree trunks and branches. As a result of this, they need excellent drainage of their potting media and they must NOT be planted in potting soil. I had a friend once that repotted a moth orchid into plain potting soil and the plant quickly died.

WHY REPOT YOUR MOTH ORCHID

Why do you need to repot your moth orchid? The potting medium will start to break down and the orchid roots will not be able to get the air and nutrients they need. Your plant will basically suffocate and start to rot.

The best time to repot a moth orchid is right after it is done flowering and you cut the bloom spike off. In order to repot your moth orchid, you'll need a few supplies:

An orchid bark mix or sphagnum moss

Clean pots with drainage holes

A bucket or a sink to soak the potting media

Scissors

PREPARING THE POTTING MEDIA

The first thing that you need to do is dump the bark mix or sphagnum moss into a bucket of hot water and let it soak for a good 30 minutes or so. The reason you want to do this is so you can properly hydrate the bark or moss so that it will accept water more easily. The bark especially needs some help to get started. Please note that sphagnum moss is NOT the same as peat moss! Peat moss will NOT work. Be sure to obtain sphagnum moss if you choose to use moss instead of bark.

CLEAN UP THE ROOTS

As your bark mix is soaking, gently take your orchid out of its pot, remove all the bark off the roots carefully, and then you'll need to cut off any dead roots.

And don't worry! You are not harming your plant! Orchids are tougher than you think. Take a pair of scissors (that have been sterilized in a flame or rubbing alcohol) and cut off any dead roots. You'll know they are dead because they may be hollow or squishy, or maybe they are completely dried up and shriveled. The roots that are alive will be firm and plump.

SELECT A NEW POT

Next, take your orchid that you've cleaned up and choose a pot that is just big enough that the roots fit in. I like to use clear plastic pots that I ordered from www.orchidsupply.com. I like clear plastic pots because I can easily assess the health of the root system. You can quickly see if anything is going wrong. In addition, you can tell how dry the potting media is so it will become easier to assess when to water.

Carefully place your orchid in the pot. Try not to harm any roots, but it is no big deal if you break one or two. Next, take the bark mix that has been soaking in water, scoop some in your hand, and place it in the pot a little at a time. If you choose to use sphagnum moss, be sure to squeeze out excess moisture out after soaking it. You're going to have to gently use your fingers or a small bamboo stick to pack the bark mix or moss into the pot. Just be gentle and work slowly. Don't leave any air gaps in the pot. You'll want to make sure that you fill in all the gaps with bark mix or sphagnum moss and that the roots are in contact with the potting media.

When you are done, give your orchid a good soaking of water in your sink to settle things, let all the excess water drain, and place it back in front of your window.

For a pictorial view on the moth orchid repotting process, I'm including a link that you can go to on my blog and visually see how I repot a moth orchid:

https://ohiotropics.com/2017/03/25/repotting-you-moth-orchid/

10 DOS IN MOTH ORCHID CARE

DO place your moth orchid on display where you can enjoy it while it is in bloom!

DO give your moth orchid enough light otherwise it will not bloom!

DO monitor your plants frequently and repot every 1-3 years.

DO fertilize your moth orchids year-round, except maybe in the winter time if it is not growing or if growth has slowed down drastically.

DO thoroughly water your orchid in the sink with tepid water.

DO summer your moth orchid outside if you can! The air circulation, temperature gradient between night and day, and rain water will do wonders for your plant!

DO inspect your plant regularly to make sure you avoid pests.

DO buy LOTS of moth orchids once you get comfortable with their care. (Sorry, I'm a plant enabler...). This way, you can have at least one that is always in bloom, like I do. I've managed to achieve this feat, and you can too!

DO provide good air circulation for your plants if you can. A ceiling fan or portable fan will work. If you can't provide this, they are still tolerant of average indoor conditions and they will not hate you too much.

DO increase humidity by using a humidifier or by setting your plants on a pebble tray to which water has been added, especially in the winter. You can also group plants together to increase humidity since plants transpire water and this will create a microclimate.

11 DON'TS IN MOTH ORCHID CARE

DON'T let your moth orchid ever sit in water for any extended period of time. It is an epiphyte and this will encourage rotting.

DON'T let any water sit in the crown of the plant or in any leaf junctions, especially if it is cooler. This will also encourage rotting.

DON'T expose your orchid to temperatures less than about 55F for long periods of time. A minimum of 55F in the Autumn evenings is OK though and this will help encourage blooming.

DON'T let your moth orchid completely dry out. It lacks the pseudobulbs that many other orchids have to store water.

DON'T put your moth orchid in full sun. These plants are not meant to grow in full sun. A reddish tinge on the leaves is an indication that the plant is at the higher end of its light tolerance. In more extreme cases, the leaves will scorch with too much sun and you will be left with a very unsightly plant.

DON'T water your orchids with ice. This is just asinine.

DON'T water your orchids with water that has been treated with a home water softening system. The resulting water contains sodium which is very toxic to plants.

DON'T rotate your plant when it is growing a new flower spike otherwise the flower stalk will grow crooked. Once you notice a flower stalk starting to grow, leave the plant in that orientation at the window and allow the flower stalk to grow towards the window.

12 PESTS

The dreaded pests! This is my least favorite topic to write about, but it is part of the inevitable reality of being a gardener! Fortunately, moth orchids aren't bothered by too many pests. I rarely have any problems with pests with my Phalaenopsis.

Before I get into some of the pests that you might encounter, let me mention a few things that you can do to prevent or minimize the severity of pest infestations:

Keeping your growing area clean and free of debris will go a long way in helping to prevent pests. Be sure to clean up any dead leaves and flowers and keep the entire growing area tidy and clean. Pests will have less places to hide!

Keep your orchids healthy by supplying them with proper growing conditions and by implementing all the cultural practices that you've learned about in this book. A healthy orchid will be much less likely to be attacked by pests than a sickly, weak orchid.

Be observant! This goes for when you purchase your plants, as well as when you are doing your routine care. If you notice any pests when you are considering purchasing a plant, don't buy the plant! If you're at home, a good time to inspect your plants is when you take them to the sink to water your moth orchids. Inspect the roots, leaves, and flowers for anything unusual.

Early detection will result in more success! You will be able to eradicate pests much more quickly and easily if you can detect and treat them before they get out of control.

So what should you be looking for? Here are some of the most common pests that you may see on your moth orchid. I have a brief description of some of the most common pests below, along with some treatment options. For a much more detailed list of orchid pests, diseases, and treatment options, check out the American Orchid Society (AOS) online. It is a treasure-trove of orchid related information.

SCALE

Scale insects appear as small, round formations, usually brown, that don't move. Scale has a hard, protective surface but are easily scraped off with your fingernail. Scale can appear anywhere on the leaves or stem of plants and can become a huge nuisance if you let it go out of control.

I lost a jade plant once that got heavily infested with scale, so early detection and treatment is key!

One way to treat scale is by dipping a Q-Tip or cotton ball into rubbing alcohol and rubbing the infected area. You can then take your finger, scrape the scale off, and then retreat the area with the rubbing alcohol.

Neem oil is also an effective, and safe way, to treat insect infestations. Follow the manufacturer's instructions for application. There are a number of harsher insecticides, but I really don't like using anything like this inside the home (or even outside for that matter!).

MEALY BUGS

Mealy bugs appear as white cottony pests on our plants, and they tend to hide in every single nook and cranny imaginable. Although you can use rubbing alcohol, similar to scale treatment, the problem is that many orchid pests can reside in the potting media as well.

You may need to take your plant out of its pot and inspect the roots to make sure that they are pest free. Earlier in this book, I mentioned my preference for using clear plastic pots to grow my orchids in. Another benefit of this practice is that you can easily see if there are any pests in the root area.

SPIDER MITES

Spider mites are one of the terrors of the plant world! I've never personally had a big issue with them on moth orchids other than seeing a little webbing here and there on flower stalks. A telltale sign that you have spider mites is seeing a fine webbing on the leaves, stems, and flower stalks.

The mites themselves are very small and appear like tiny specks. In severe cases, if they attack the leaves, you'll see a mottled discoloration of the leaves. I've had more severe issues with spider mites on other plants, but orchids can get them too. I normally take a moistened paper towel and wipe the leaves, including the undersides. The resulting paper towel will be a yellowish color. Spider mites are more of a problem when humidity is low, especially during the winter if you have forced air heat.

Besides wiping the leaves down with a damp paper towel or sponge, rinsing off your plants regularly will help control the population. Keep repeating this regularly and over time, it will improve. Also, if you move your plants outside during the warm months, this will also help control the situation. Spider mites hate moisture so if you can provide high humidity and regularly rinse your plants off and wipe them clean, this will go a long way in helping to control spider mites.

CLOSING THOUGHTS ON TREATMENT

For any of the treatment methods described above, I like to take my plants outside if possible (weather and temperature permitting) so I'm not making a mess indoors. This also helps minimize the risk of dislodging pests and spreading to other plants.

If you can't bring the plant outside, take your plant to a wash tub, sink or other area away from other plants. I do prefer using treatment methods like rubbing alcohol, neem oil, or other safe and low toxicity treatment methods. For our own safety, and the safety of our families and pets, I use synthetic insecticides only as a last resort, if ever.

In really bad cases, I might just throw the plant away. Unless it is a rare or unusual specimen, it may not be worth the trouble or exposure to chemicals.

Of course, there are many other varieties of pests, but the ones I've described are some of the most common ones. Moth orchids are generally pretty pest free in general.

13 CONCLUSION

This concludes Moth Orchid Mastery! I hope that you have enjoyed reading this book and please leave me a review on Amazon. I would highly appreciate it! This book is my first of a series of eBooks and paperbacks that I plan on publishing related to houseplants. I am very passionate about growing a large variety of houseplants, and am making it my mission to explain things in a way that is easy to understand and practical for the general masses.

I hope this book has given you the knowledge, confidence and enthusiasm to help you demystify orchid growing. Once you realize that they are not difficult to grow at all, they become addictive and can become quite an obsession! So beware!

Finally, please don't forget to visit my houseplant blog site at www.ohiotropics.com where I regularly write various articles on the care of a large variety of houseplants. You can easily subscribe by email as well. I send all my subscribers regular communication emails every time I have a new blog post or have special news to share.

You can also find me on Instagram (@ohiotropics) where I post daily, inspirational and informative houseplant care photos and tips.

I wish you the best of luck in your moth orchid journey and if you have any questions at all, I am here to help! You can reach me at theohiotropics@gmail.com.

14 TESTIMONIALS

The following are a few testimonials for Ohio Tropics on both moth orchid care, and houseplant care in general:

"As a Horticulturalist, I am truly inspired and impressed with Raffaele's remarkable plant blog at www.ohiotropics.com. Ohio Tropics has enriched the plant community through factual information, knowledge, and understanding of plant care, as well as providing a place they can go to learn something new."

Marisa Reyes in Wisconsin

"I have never been able to rebloom an orchid by simply following the tag on my store purchased orchids. A friend recommended Raffaele, and I immediately began scanning his blog for info on orchids. I now realize why my orchids were not reblooming. I ditched the ice cube watering system that is somehow still all over the web and began following Raffaele's instructions. Within weeks, I had a new flower spike! My plants are thriving, and I am a happy camper. Thank you, Ohio Tropics!"

Jackie in Winchester, Virginia

"Not only do I have a black thumb but I travel frequently and have a cat. I didn't think it was possible to grow *anything* in my house. Raffaele helped me to understand that orchids are not intimidating. In fact, they are quite robust and require very little attention. I would highly recommend his advice and this book. If I can get an orchid to re-bloom you can too!"

Meredith in Cleveland, Ohio

"Ohio Tropics changed the way I water all of my plants, and they're happier for it! He's so helpful, positive, and fun to follow!"

Bethany in Michigan

"I needed help with my Pilea that was curling its leaves and not growing. I reached out to Raffaele in hopes of receiving some advice from a person I love following on Instagram. Within an hour he responded and gave me advice! I was surprised and thrilled that he was so open to talking to someone he had never met and offered amazing advice on how to help out my Pilea! Within a week my Pilea has completely changed and even has 3 new leaves! Thank you so much!!"

Melannie in Orlando, Florida

"I stumbled upon Ohio Tropics' Instagram [@ohiotropics] account back in January 2018. I was struggling with my plant collection and desperately needed some guidance. Raffaele helped me rehab my prayer plant that went into terrible shock because I purchased it on the coldest day and didn't think to protect it from the elements as I put it in the car. Months it took, but Raffaele talked me through it and I felt supported. I felt the same support when I was struggling with my Croton. He was there to help. Now my Croton is so happy that she is blooming. He even gave me the push I needed to experiment with leaf propagating my Sansevieria. Which so far has been successful. Even watching him train his Pothos on a moss pole inspired me to do the same. He's helped me identify half a dozen plants that I was either gifted or just had to have but had no clue what they were. Honestly, my collection nor my confidence would be where it's at today without Ohio Tropics. I am forever grateful."

Cole in Albany, New York

"I saw a lot of 'urban jungle' pictures on Pinterest and was totally in love, so when I moved into a new place I knew what I wanted. I bought my first plant this January and it kept living! After a few months I bought my second, and soon came the third, fourth etc…but no one around me has a green thumb. So I searched a lot online and found a Dutch website with a lot of care tips but I still found it difficult. When I stumbled upon your Instagram [@ohiotropics] and website [www.ohiotropics.com] I found one article which I live by now: The Absolute Best Thing You Can Do For Your Houseplants. The insights in here made things so simple for me as a total newbee. So thank you for your blog and Instagram! I love love love reading about anything houseplant related, and especially from someone with much more experience than me."

Lotte in the Netherlands

"No matter who you are, an old school gardener, long time expert, stubborn newcomer, doesn't matter…everyone can get stuck in their ways. I think informative posts like the ones you've continued making can help everyone. It's always solid information, never some goofy trick or hack or shortcut, and that's what this community needs more of; clear, concise information and someone to help provide clear explanations of why we apply the methods we do in the home garden."

Rusty in Michigan

"I was lucky enough to come across Ohio Tropics recently after I bought my first houseplant and I have since bought many more. The tips on watering, choosing which pot to use, and how much light the plants want have helped them to thrive in my home but behind all of that is an obvious passion for plants that he is more than happy to share with others."

Will in London, UK

ABOUT THE AUTHOR

Raffaele Di Lallo is the founder of Ohio Tropics and helps tens of thousands of people learn how to grow houseplants through his daily tips on Instagram and his blog site at www.ohiotropics.com. He has a very large and rapidly growing follower base on Instagram and can be found @ohiotropics.

His blog site, www.ohiotropics.com, has rapidly grown in popularity and was named one of the top 25 houseplant blogs on the internet according to www.feedspot.com. His blog site has readers in over 100 countries and posts primarily about houseplant care.

Besides being a lifetime gardener, he received his Certificate of Home Horticulture from the Oregon State University as a part of their Master Gardener program, completed a Green Gardener program at the Cleveland Botanical Gardens, and is a member of the American Orchid Society. Raffaele earned a B.S. in Chemical Engineering from Northwestern University in Evanston, IL.

Raffaele has been interviewed for multiple podcasts, including On the Ledge, hosted by the venerable Jane Perrone in the U.K. He has also been a guest blogger on numerous sites and has written for www.gardeningknowhow.com. His enthusiasm for gardening and houseplants is infectious and has inspired countless individuals both locally and around the world.

Made in the USA
San Bernardino, CA
25 April 2020

68528188R00022